Heroes

Heroes

LEGO® BUILDERS CHANGING OUR WORLD—ONE BRICK AT A TIME

Graham E. Hancock

CHRONICLE BOOKS
SAN FRANCISCO

Library of Congress Cataloging-in-Publication Data is available.

ISBN 978-1-4521-8233-9

Manufactured in China.

MIX
Paper | Supporting responsible forestry
FSC™ C008047

Design by MacFadden & Thorpe.

10 9 8 7 6 5 4 3 2 1

See the full range of LEGO® books and gifts at
www.chroniclebooks.com/LEGO.

Chronicle books and gifts are available at special quantity discounts to corporations, professional associations, literacy programs, and other organizations. For details and discount information, please contact our premiums department at corporatesales@chroniclebooks.com or at 1-800-759-0190.

Chronicle Books LLC
680 Second Street
San Francisco, California 94107
www.chroniclebooks.com

CONTENTS

FOREWORD

One of the things I've always loved about LEGO® play is that it can be anything you want it to be. Take a pile of bricks, with no set and no instructions, and just watch where your imagination takes you. As you'll see in this book, it can take you to some extraordinary places.

Here, you'll meet twelve visionary builders who have turned LEGO play into life-altering innovations through the power of their curiosity, creativity, and passion. Our LEGO heroes come from across the globe, from Canada to Colombia, from Europe to Singapore, and from a zoo in Maryland to a music college in Istanbul. They are scientists, designers, teachers, psychologists, artists, vets, musicians. Some are specialists in play, sustainability, or social responsibility at the LEGO Group; others are lifelong LEGO fans. All share a drive to make the world a better place and inspire the builders of tomorrow.

Each one of these stories amazes me. I'm blown away by the optimism, originality, and sheer generosity of spirit demonstrated by our building heroes. They illustrate something that gets to the heart of our philosophy of Learning through Play.

Our heroes start with an ambition to solve a problem, such as how to support a turtle's fractured shell (tricky) or how to restore a coral reef (verging on impossible). They approach their challenge with a playful attitude and a handful of LEGO bricks, asking themselves, '"What if?," "Why not?" and "How might that work?"

Thanks to the LEGO® System in Play, all the bricks from different sets fit together, offering endless variety and unlimited potential. Our heroes experiment and explore. They build, unbuild, and rebuild. Their playful approach allows them to leapfrog over obstacles and arrive at dazzling and unexpected new possibilities.

This is how a veterinary student at Maryland Zoo invents a LEGO wheelchair for a seriously injured turtle. It's also what inspires researchers at the National University of Singapore to grow coral on LEGO in an aquarium, in an experiment to produce coral stocks more sustainably.

Looking at the inventions on these pages, I find it heartwarming that so many LEGO builders are drawn to help people who face exclusion. I'm thinking of wheelchair ramps that make our streets more accessible, prosthetics for people living with limb loss, activities for seniors with dementia, play for neurodivergent children, and Braille Bricks for children with visual impairments.

This resonates with everything we're doing at the LEGO Group to support sustainability —taking action to create a lasting positive impact on society and the environment. Our LEGO heroes are part of a global community who are discovering real-world applications for what was originally designed as a child's toy. Every day I hear about more inspiring people who are using their talent and love of LEGO to change the world for the better. Let's celebrate all these heroes. They're building a bridge to the future, one brick at a time.

—Tim Brooks, Vice President of Environmental Responsibility
  at the LEGO Group

INTRODUCTION

Anything is possible with LEGO® bricks. Through the LEGO System in Play—where all LEGO elements are compatible with one another—your creativity is boundless, your imagination is limitless, and your play is endless. These elements are an amazingly innovative medium that allow you to build a castle, a pirate ship, or even something yet to be imagined, all using the same pile of bricks. With the LEGO system, a dash of creativity, and an unwavering spirit, anyone can become a hero—one brick at a time.

LEGO® *Heroes* shares twelve examples of people who used the LEGO brick beyond its initial purpose, making a connection between a small element and a big idea. This spark of an idea has the potential to make the world a better—and more colorful—place. These builders see the LEGO brick as not just a toy, but a source of never-ending creative potential.

As children, we see opportunities to be creative everywhere without even realizing it. If something is out of reach, we find a chair to stand on. If we want a world for our toys, we commandeer a cardboard box. If we feel compelled to make music, we bang together a ladle and saucepan. Our solutions may not work on the first attempt, but then we try something else—and we keep trying—until we succeed. This tenacity in seeking solutions in creative and innovative ways is embodied by the everyday heroes whose stories are told in this book.

Veterinarians who help a turtle to walk again, an inventor designing prosthetics focused on the needs of children, a creative thinker providing resources for neurodivergent children—the individuals and organizations featured in this book bring awareness to the potential for change and for new thinking using brick-based solutions. Although LEGO bricks may seem small and simple on their own, when they are clicked together to work in tandem, they create something that can change our world.

Meanwhile, the LEGO System in Play itself also embodies the spirit of innovation. It shows that a handful of disparate elements—made fifty years ago or yesterday—can be combined to become something greater than they are individually, an example of the way that proactive thinkers often take seemingly unconnected concepts and put them together to produce a novel solution to a problem. No matter what your area of interest, where your skill set lies, or what kind of thinker you are, you can use your passion and your ingenuity to innovate and help the people in your community.

As the editor of *Blocks*, a monthly magazine celebrating creativity with LEGO bricks, I am fortunate to meet people from all over the world who are doing incredible things with LEGO bricks. People are always using these elements in new and surprising ways—and every time you think you've heard about the most original use, you can be sure someone else is doing something entirely different and unexpected. When I speak to someone using the LEGO System in a unique and innovative way, I feel energized and inspired.

It is because of this excitement that I am so delighted to bring you these stories. As you turn the pages you'll be inspired by people from around the globe of all ages and backgrounds who are building a better world in ways big and small. Whether they are finding a practical solution to a tricky problem, proving a concept that will help people live better lives, or simply making the world a more joyful place, these heroes demonstrate the creative spirit and potential found in every LEGO brick.

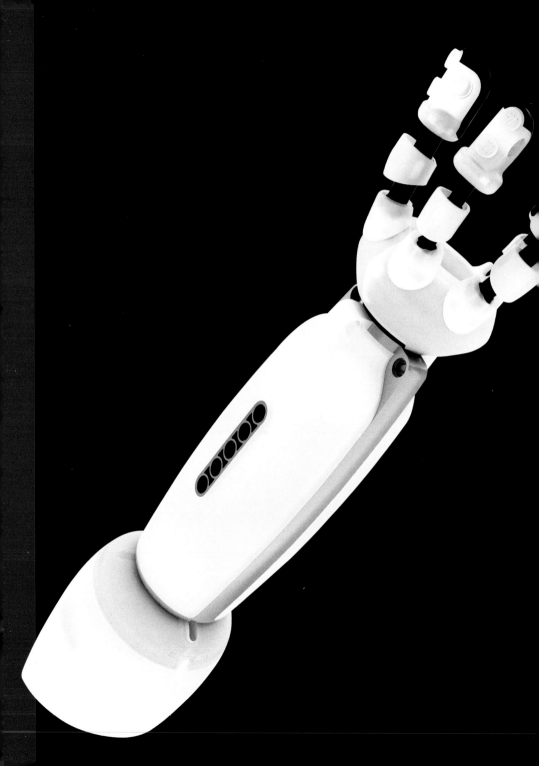

CHAPTER 01

The Future of Pros- thetics

CARLOS ARTURO TORRES'S
CUSTOMIZABLE SYSTEM

Carlos Arturo Torres knew he wanted to help the people of his home country of Colombia living with limb loss, many of whom were victims of decades of armed conflict throughout the country. However, it wasn't until he met Dario, an eight-year-old boy born without a right forearm, and a partnership with the LEGO Future Lab that Carlos's mission crystalized.

Dario, also from Colombia, met Carlos through CIREC, a nonprofit working on the rehabilitation of people with physical disabilities, many of whom are children with limb loss. "As a Colombian citizen, I've seen the bad things that the armed conflict has left behind," says Carlos. While working on his master's degree in product design, he resolved to develop a customized prosthetic system for children and contacted Dario to gain a deeper understanding of the experience of a child living with limb loss.

Carlos spent time with Dario to get a sense of how the youngster lived, visiting with his family and joining him at his school. "When I started my research in Colombia, I noticed a sketch that Dario made. It was a robot with lots of arms and gear, including a 'laser eye,'" Carlos says. "Dario explained that the laser eye was made by the robot himself because he was the only one who knew what he needed. I realized the [prosthetic] project was not just about customization but also about creating your own devices." This insight contributed to the body of research that Carlos was building. He recognized that children know their own needs best and that every child is different. As prosthetics tend to be modular, it would make sense for children to be able to build their own modules to attach to their prosthesis, adapting the artificial limb to the needs of each child.

ABOVE The IKO system is designed to spark the imagination of the child—a prosthesis can become a digger.

ABOVE There's a space for a minifigure on the charging station, so even the accessories can be customized.

ABOVE Carlos worked closely with Dario to understand his needs, spending time with the whole family.

"We have a user-centered approach for every project. This means that everything we do must be meaningful and useful for people."

While exploring different ways to engage children in his project, Carlos saw a natural connection between his child-oriented customizable prosthetic system and the mechanism that allows LEGO® bricks to click together. By integrating LEGO elements into the prosthetics, it would give children both functionality and an opportunity to explore their own creativity in a playful, social, and inclusive way. Drawing on Dario's initial inspiration, Carlos approached the LEGO Future Lab for assistance in making his system, which he eventually named IKO, compatible with LEGO elements.

Carlos was a student at Umeå Institute of Design, a Swedish university, when he embarked on the project that would become IKO. "At the institute,"

he explains, "we have a user-centered approach for every project. This means that everything we do must be meaningful and useful for people. Once I started the project, I realized that there are needs for kids beyond their physical needs. Kids need to develop socially, emotionally, and physically all together." Of course, their physical needs must be addressed, but psychologically they must also learn to deal with the life changes they face living with limb loss.

For the next stage in the development of IKO, Carlos traveled to Billund, Denmark, to visit the LEGO headquarters, where he received a crash course in LEGO building with the Master Builder Academy sets. "During my time in Future Lab, I noticed how awesomely creative the LEGO® System is. Fans around the world create fantastic things, and the LEGO System gives you the possibility to make almost anything you want," Carlos says.

FACING PAGE Dario tests out a prototype IKO prosthesis.

"My main objective with the project was to empower children to create amazing stuff, and the LEGO System was the perfect platform for it."

The LEGO System allowed for the endless creativity that Carlos sought. Every LEGO element is carefully designed so that it fits with the rest of the portfolio. Carlos spent time designing and testing different approaches to a modular prosthetic compatible with LEGO bricks. His design needed to balance creative expression and practicality. He wanted a product that worked for children, that they could easily manipulate, and that incorporated the LEGO element connection points.

To that end, the charging station for the prosthetic's battery has two studs on one corner, the perfect space to personalize the prosthetic with a LEGO minifigure. The battery itself is combined with the socket and the muscle module contains an integrated LEGO® MINDSTORMS® motor, with spaces for LEGO® Technic pins to be connected around the module to allow building in any direction. The hand offers multiple types of grips for different activities. Even the fingers have LEGO studs on the end to allow for further customization. However, he also took into consideration that giving the child too much freedom in the customization of the prosthesis would limit its use in day-to-day life.

In addition to including studs on the prosthetic so children could connect bricks to it, Carlos incorporated the ethos of the LEGO System—the modularity, the ease of use, and the ability to constantly make changes—in the design. Specially designed connectors are simply pushed and twisted into place. The simplicity of the attachment method was key to making the prosthesis as intuitive to use as classic LEGO bricks. "One of the big features of the LEGO System in Play is that it is a social toy," Carlos explains. "You can play on your own, but you can also play with your siblings, your parents, your friends, and even make friends while playing with it. By integrating this feature in the project, something really cool happened. While we were building together with Dario and his family, he became the lead builder. He could give instructions to all of us on how to build everything. When we finished, the pride of creation was different this time; we all made something that was in his arm, and we were all as happy as him when he was able to use it."

After Carlos developed IKO, it was exhibited at the Ars Electronica Center in Austria and he won several awards for his advances in modular prosthetics. However, like many innovative ideas ahead of their time, this particular design did not make it to market. But Carlos is pleased to see his work inspired several companies to explore lower-cost modular prosthetics that offer people more flexibility, an iteration of his idea that will eventually become a reality. The project is a message to people and the prosthetics industry, raising awareness about the importance of caring for children without limbs in creative and thoughtful ways.

FACING PAGE Dario and his minifigure friend.

CHAPTER 02

LEGO®
Replay

GIVING LEGO® BRICKS A SECOND LIFE

Many children have experienced the joy of digging into a bin of LEGO® bricks in search of the perfect element—containers briming with new elements together with those passed down from older siblings, friends ready to rehome their collection, or even parents and grandparents who played with them as children. Some children turn to new interests as they get older, leaving less time for brick-building pursuits. At this point, an average toy may be discarded or neglected. However, LEGO bricks are often saved from this particular fate. Perhaps it is because LEGO owners recognize the durability and longevity of their bricks, or maybe they want to minimize what they contribute to landfills, or perhaps, for many, this timeless toy inspires nostalgic feelings of freedom and creativity. Whatever the reason, LEGO bricks are the perfect hand-me-down to be passed from child to child and generation to generation, in large part because of the LEGO® System in Play.

"The LEGO System in Play means that all elements fit together, can be used in multiple ways, can be built together," said Godtfred Kirk Christiansen, the son of the LEGO Group founder, Ole Kirk Kristiansen, who pioneered the System during the 1950s and '60s. "This means that bricks bought years ago will fit perfectly with bricks bought in the future," a reason that encourages builders to hold on to their decades-old bricks so they can be used later.

In fact, Godtfred's strategy seems to be working because the LEGO Group

ABOVE Whether LEGO bricks are brand new or reconditioned, they offer the same opportunities for creativity.

data shows that 98 percent of consumers don't throw away LEGO bricks, and more than 50 percent of LEGO owners pass bricks on to friends, families, or charities. Although for those who don't have children, grandchildren, or a neighbor to share them with, there's not always a clear path to pass them down—that is, until the LEGO Group saw an opportunity to build a creative system to pass on these endlessly shareable bricks.

LEGO® Replay is a program for people to donate their much-loved LEGO bricks and share the power of play with children in need across the United States and Canada. Because official LEGO elements made as far back as the 1950s and '60s still click with bricks made today, brick donations can be cleaned, boxed up, and sent to children who could use more play in their lives. As well as making sure bricks don't end up in landfills, this program gives children who wouldn't otherwise have access to these playful resources opportunities to problem solve, collaborate, and think creatively.

The original idea came from the primary users of LEGO bricks—children. Letters and emails came from youngsters who did not want to contribute to the world's global waste crisis by throwing away their old elements, but who were also ready for their elements to find a new home. "A lot of our ideas are inspired by children; they really challenge us to think and do better," says Lauren O'Hara, director of circular business models at the LEGO Group and a member of the LEGO Replay team.

Godtfred's guiding ethos of the LEGO System in Play also supports the LEGO Group sustainability mission, which is

integral to their business today. Underpinning LEGO Replay is the concept of a circular economy—the idea that the economy should be structured so existing resources are reused to minimize waste in order to create a sustainable future, rather than a system that continually uses new resources. Companies with a strong sustainability agenda, like the LEGO Group, are working to incorporate circularity into their business models and also teach future generations about the model.

While this economic concept originated some time ago and is increasing in popularity, the steps the Replay team learned to put this idea into action were unique. When it comes to gathering used LEGO bricks and reconditioning them, there's no off-the-shelf solution, so they enlisted the help of Monika Wiela, the

ABOVE Reconditioned LEGO Replay bricks are reaching children who might not otherwise have access to LEGO elements.

founder of the nonprofit program, Give Back Box Charity Inc., a US-based organization that allows consumers to send items they are no longer using to charities that will then pass them on to people in need. "She introduced us to a lot of companies in the world that are out there helping to eliminate waste from overproduction," Lauren explains. "We started working with a couple different production companies and a couple different partners to help us understand how to take things back, how to process them in a way that creates a safe and fun [re-homed] product at the end."

The process of sharing LEGO bricks through LEGO Replay is easy. If you are based in a participating region, visit the LEGO Replay website, *www.LEGO.com/ Replay*, and print out a free shipping label. Pack up the bricks, label the box, and drop it in the mail—it will then find its way to the Replay team, who will do the rest. Since the program launched in the United States in 2019 and in Canada in 2020, they have already donated brick boxes to more than 117,000 children, extending the life of approximately 133 million bricks. Over the years the process has become more streamlined, but the team continues to seek ways to support the circular mission of the LEGO Group by continuously improving the processes for brick sharing. "Our goal is to get as many bricks as we possibly can and ensure that they can be passed on. We're just trying to make it better and better, faster and faster," Lauren sums up.

RIGHT All LEGO System elements are compatible with each other, no matter when they were produced.

A LEGO Replay programmatic challenge is when things other than LEGO bricks or elements are shared in donated boxes. Over the years, the LEGO brick bin can become a place where other toys, stray shirt buttons, pen caps, and other misplaced items wind up. Sometimes, unsorted bins that go straight to the Replay team often still contain these random items. To minimize non-brick donations, the website now explicitly explains what can and can't be donated. Once the bricks arrive to be processed and shared, they are put through a rigorous cleaning. The Replay team spent more than a year developing the optimal processing method with support from the LEGO Group safety and quality team to ensure that the LEGO bricks being passed on are up to the company's safety standards. Once the bricks are cleaned and repackaged, the boxes, each containing more than 1,000 elements, are ready to be shared and to provide endless hours of creativity and joy.

The LEGO Group wants to leave a positive impact on the world for children to inherit. In part this is done through their social responsibility team, including LEGO Replay, and their engagement with a number of charity partners that support children in need. "We work with the Build the Change program in the United States, where children can learn about the circular

ABOVE Millions of bricks have been rehomed with the help of LEGO Replay.

"Partly LEGO Replay is here to be an inspiration to you to do better with items you no longer want."

economy and learn that the best way to help the planet is to reuse things over and over and over again if you possibly can. We also let them use a mix of bricks and elements that are renewed so they can see that a renewed brick is just the same as a new brick," Lauren explains.

In another partnership, during the lockdowns put in place in response to the COVID-19 pandemic, the company provided LEGO Replay bricks to children who did not have access to them during home learning. "We found a lot of children went home to houses that didn't have the materials that they needed," Lauren recalls. "The LEGO Group partnered with schools across Connecticut and Massachusetts to provide Replay brick boxes for children who were learning at home." After bricks were distributed through the schools, the Replay team worked with teachers to create a curriculum integrating LEGO bricks to encourage learning through play. For example, some teachers used LEGO bricks as creative prompts for writing exercises about animal habitats.

LEGO Replay builds on a longstanding tradition of sharing LEGO bricks. LEGO bricks offer endless creativity and joy for the builders of tomorrow, and passing on LEGO bricks ensures a new builder can experience the joy of creation. The LEGO Group is exploring how to expand LEGO Replay and other new circular concepts in more countries, but one doesn't need to wait for LEGO Replay to be available in their own country—LEGO bricks are so easily shareable. Lauren explains, "Partly LEGO Replay is here to be an inspiration to you to do better with items you no longer want; to use them more effectively, to seek to repair, [rather than replace]. Our goal is to tell you about LEGO Replay, and hopefully it inspires you to pass LEGO bricks on to children in need in your own way."

CHAPTER 03

Urban Art

JAN VORMANN ON MAKING A MORE COLORFUL WORLD

Keep your eyes peeled the next time you are walking around Paris, Venice, Budapest, or Madrid; there's a chance you might see colorful little LEGO® bricks filling the gaps in centuries-old walls. You're likely to wonder how they got there. Throughout these cities and many more around the world, LEGO elements are patching up missing mortar and grout lost to time as part of artist Jan Vormann's playful street art project, Dispatchwork.

Jan has always been interested in simple objects. Much of his work focuses on ludic objects—items that are purely playful in nature, like dice. "They can carry a lot of meaning," he explains. "Dice are about probabilities, but also about chance and luck." Given his interest in simple but playful objects, it's no surprise that LEGO bricks caught his attention. What is innovative about his work, though, is that he places these elements outside, where one might least expect them. Typically, LEGO bricks are found inside the home, so being confronted with these bright pops of color out in the world can feel novel and pleasantly surprising.

"I wanted to do something that would visually look like graffiti, but it's not vandalism, it's the repair process, done with a certain care," Jan recalls. His first opportunity to execute the concept was in Bocchignano, a small village in Italy, where he was invited to present a street art installation. The juxtaposition between brick and stone walls worn down by centuries and the colorful, modern, and precise lines created by the LEGO bricks highlights a moment where history meets modernity. The artist saw a connection between the historic buildings and

LEGO bricks—how they had been built over time with what was available, often in a way that was unplanned.

The German artist now travels the world patching up holes with LEGO bricks. Over the years he has added a splash of color and playfulness to dozens of towns and cities, visiting many European cities, as well as locations in North America, South America, and Asia. Jan is conscious of the fact that when he is invited to present his work in other places around the world, he doesn't know the locality. That's why he explores the town he is in. Although he has a practical need to find locations to present his installations, he also wants to get a sense of

ABOVE LEGO bricks fill in gaps in a wall in the village of Bocchignano, Italy.

FACING PAGE Jan, seen here, travels all over the world with LEGO bricks, looking for cracks in walls wherever he goes.

"I wanted to do something that would visually look like graffiti, but it's not vandalism, it's the repair process, done with a certain care."

the neighborhoods. He then patches the walls with LEGO bricks right there on the street, inviting conversations with local people who are curious about what he is doing.

What makes the patches so appealing is that they predominantly use the common LEGO bricks that anyone would recognize. By using those familiar elements in their traditional bright colors, Jan provides an immediate connection to many people's childhoods. However, just because the patches have a childlike appearance and are not structurally integral to the wall doesn't mean that they are simple to create. "I take one by eights and two by eights that are right for the depths of the hole and try to encompass the slopes, the upward slopes, the downward slopes, for any elevation or any change of direction in the hole. I don't

cut the bricks, and I don't squeeze them too much. I try to go organically around the shape and find the perfect form. It's a little bit of a challenge to know the different shapes, especially the different slopes, that exist and also to estimate the straight line, so that it ends up flush with the wall."

That's not to say that there aren't a few special elements and surprises built into what Jan creates. "I try to implement interesting moments where people can look over the work and have a different experience each time, because there are always little details that maybe escaped the eye before. I try to put boxes or little doors that people can peek behind, and sometimes there is a little room behind it. I always want to make little moments so the curious are rewarded."

Initially, Jan created the Dispatchwork installations entirely on his own. "Then in Berlin, we were standing at a wall where there are a lot of bullets and shrapnel holes. People were stopping by, asking what we were doing. I started to just

ABOVE Dispatchworks is a participatory project; people can either fill in gaps in walls independently or join Jan as he constructs these colorful patches.

hand out bricks and people began to participate. And this is how that branch of the project developed, from basically just inviting people." After that experience, he started to set up workshops where he would invite people to join him, instead of exploring the locations on his own. People could come along, grab a bunch of LEGO bricks, and start patching up the walls. It's a little more complex than it may seem, as the constructions have to not only fit the gap precisely but also be built in a very solid way, so they fit snugly and avoid falling to the ground.

"When I go somewhere and make a workshop, a lot of people think 'Ah, yeah, for the kids.' But a lot of times the parents, especially boomers and millennials, have a very deep connection with this toy. A patch can take up to at least thirty minutes and then it goes upwards of seven, eight hours if you want. But kids do not always have the patience. A lot of times, it's actually the parents who would finish the hole, whereas the kids would do a little bit here and there."

Putting art in front of people and getting that immediate reaction is why Jan likes creating in public spaces. It ensures that the art is claiming a space in society, rather than requiring people to come and find it. All street art is participatory in that sense, but Dispatchwork went a step further. After getting people involved through workshops, Jan encouraged others to build wall patches in their own communities.

Using LEGO bricks as a medium was universally understood by people around the world, and many were keen to participate. "I was always traveling and trying to find these objects that are readable and understandable in many different contexts. The brick is one of those things—this project can be understood in Japan, China, South America, Africa, Europe, and the United States. If there is a global culture, then LEGO bricks would be part of it. There are some things that are culturally intrinsic, and we share them with the largest amount of people worldwide."

Jan started to receive photographs from people who had been inspired by his work, leading him to set up the *www.Dispatchwork.info* website. There, anyone can upload photos of where they have added some color to patch up a hole. To convey that universality, there are no country names on the map when you visit his website—there are only markers that show where people have patched up a gap. From New York to Taipei, Jan's work inspires people around the world to take a handful of LEGO bricks to create their own art and bring some brightness to their communities.

FACING PAGE Filling in gaps with LEGO elements is trickier than it sounds. Jan has good knowledge of slope and arch pieces, which comes in handy when working around irregular shapes.

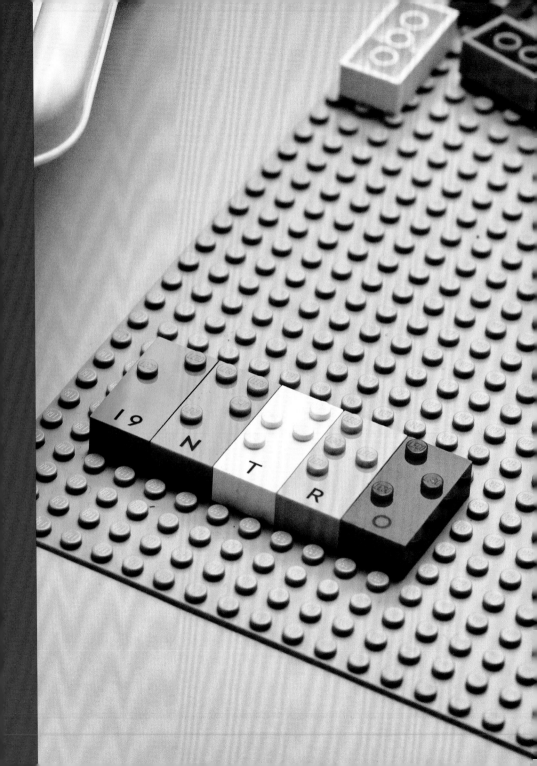

CHAPTER 04

LEGO® Braille Bricks

LEARNING THROUGH PLAY

The braille code of touch reading and writing has been around for two hundred years, serving an important purpose in the lives of people with visual impairments. At a time when braille was at risk of feeling dated and out of step with modern technology, the LEGO Group began to investigate a big idea: bricks with studs that correspond with the braille code.

Imagine a LEGO® brick made up of six studs—then take away some of those studs so that the new stud pattern represents a braille character. This simple change to the world's most iconic toy enables it to help teach children with visual impairments to read.

"We were, over a number of years, contacted by various blind organizations encouraging us to look into this opportunity because it's such an obvious fit," says Stine Storm, senior play and health specialist at the LEGO Foundation. "We simply didn't have a natural fit within the organization. But the LEGO Foundation

launched a department called New Ventures." The LEGO Foundation owns 25 percent of the LEGO Group, with that share in the company providing the organization with the resources to help children around the world receive better access to learning through play. Now, children with vision impairments are benefiting directly from the LEGO Foundation's work.

Developed by Louis Braille in the 1800s, braille is a code that can be read by touching patterns of raised dots that represent letters and symbols. In 2018 Stine and her colleagues started looking into the potential of a LEGO® Braille Bricks concept. "We weren't the experts in braille, so we joined forces with a lot of blind organizations," she explains. One such organization was the United Kingdom's Royal National Institute of Blind People (RNIB). "There comes a certain point in a child's education, where if their vision is so poor or completely absent, print is no longer viable in terms of the size that you would need it to be. We would at that point introduce braille," says RNIB principal education officer Caireen Sutherland. "Braille is easier taught when children are younger, when they're more adaptable, when they've got better tactile skills."

"That said, learning braille is really, really challenging," she continues. "Even when you start young, there are so many skills that are needed. Everything is based on a configuration of those six dots. It's pretty mind-blowing and complicated— especially if you're teaching that to a child who is only just of reading age."

Because young children are better equipped to learn braille and also at the

ABOVE Each box of LEGO Braille Bricks is donated free of charge to community organizations.

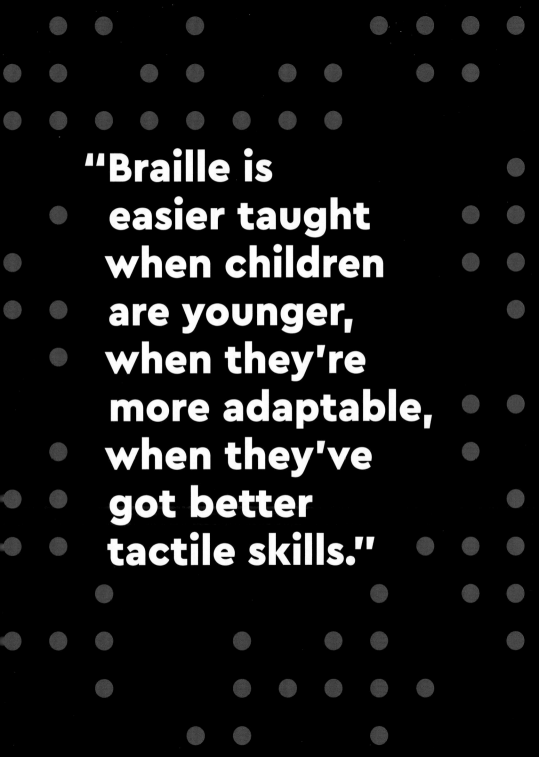

"Braille is easier taught when children are younger, when they're more adaptable, when they've got better tactile skills."

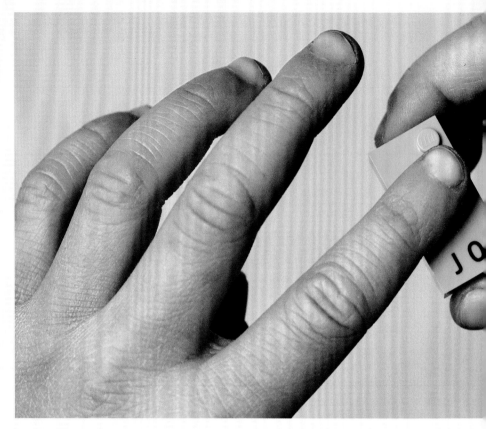

ABOVE A classic LEGO brick provides the template, but studs are strategically placed to represent a specific letter in braille.

perfect age for LEGO bricks, this over-lapping moment offers a real opportunity to combine the learning of a needed skill with a sense of joy and playfulness. For children, "experience shows that if you know braille, you have a higher likelihood of going on to further education and becoming self-sufficient," says Stine. "That's why we want to focus on children, so they are not left behind, so that they obtain these abilities and follow their desires. The purpose is to give them the agency to do what they want." And if they are having fun while doing it, that's an added bonus.

"The critical thing for me is that a lot of learning is done as a child through play," says RNIB director of services David Clarke. "This isn't about being sat behind a book or the lessons I used to have." Educators have been frustrated for years by a lack of new resources for teaching

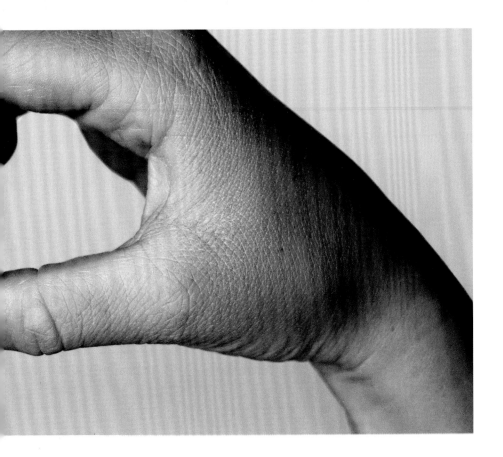

and learning braille; many of the existing options were quite dated, unchanged from decades ago. For the RNIB, LEGO bricks have the cool factor that old-fashioned resources were missing.

Organizations, like RNIB, were carefully selected by the LEGO Foundation to reach as many children as possible around the world. In different countries, blind organizations are distributing the sets of bricks. Rather than sending them to individuals, the organizations send the boxes to schools and community groups where they can be enjoyed by different children over time. "LEGO bricks don't wear out. You can use them generation after generation," Stine explains. "We wanted to ensure that's the case here because this LEGO project is not-for-profit. No teachers are paying for the teaching materials or the tool kits."

"Braille Bricks offer that inclusion so you can now do early-stage braille skills as a group."

Getting the physical LEGO bricks manufactured was a logistical challenge; for every new LEGO element that is produced in the company's expansive manufacturing centers, a new mold must be made. For each new stud arrangement on the brick, there had to be a new mold, and then the relevant letter or number had to be printed on the correct brick. Given the aim was to offer LEGO Braille Bricks to children around the world, the manufacturing process is expanding even more with variations in different languages.

But while the LEGO Braille Bricks are at the heart of the concept, teaching is not just about having a tool. That tool must be used in a way that can communicate something to the learner, and along with each set delivered to a school, a corresponding curriculum of play-based activities is provided. It didn't take long, though, for teachers to go beyond what the LEGO Foundation had provided. "As with anything, you put things in the hands of people who are born to teach, and they will find the most unbelievable, imaginative uses for them," David says.

Teachers are collaborating online to share best practices and discuss new ways that LEGO Braille Bricks can be used. An activity might involve building a sandwich by picking out the first letter of each ingredient, or students might use the bricks to spell out their name, then

add other bricks perpendicularly to turn it into an acronym.

"When we started doing math, one of the teachers got hold of the bricks and just produced this amazing scheme of work. It has been brilliant to see people being innovative and making the learning experience exciting."

Moreover, LEGO Braille Bricks allow young people with visual impairments to learn alongside their peers. The initial prototype featured both print and braille to encourage inclusivity. "We included print on bricks so that you can teach both a sighted child and a blind child alongside each other," Stine explains. "The twenty-first-century skills like communication, collaboration, joint problem-solving, creative thinking—all these things happen when you get children together. That's when the magic happens—when they start collaborating and all these amazing ideas come up." By having print on a brick, sighted children can identify the symbol that the brick represents, while children with vision impairments can use the pattern of studs to identify it.

FACING PAGE The LEGO Foundation provides resources and lesson plans alongside the physical bricks for teachers to use in their classrooms.

ABOVE Letters are printed on LEGO Braille Bricks so children with visual impairments and sighted children can learn together.

David considers this to be a game changer. "A lot of this learning will be through play, enjoyment, and fun, and not a special skill that you have to learn because you're blind. It will make it a completely normal experience within the classroom." He also recalls, "I remember being dragged off to typing lessons. I never forget the time that my typing class clashed with the first launch of the space shuttle, and I was like, 'Really? I've got to go and type?' I was being dragged out of something to go and do something special."

A situation like this, Caireen adds, "risks a horrible isolation, social issues with your peer group, [and] a lack of opportunity to take part in lots of key activities when you're young. Braille Bricks offer that inclusion so you can now do early-stage braille skills as a group, when before that wasn't ever an option because you needed a whole load of adults there to translate. It's less powerful as soon as an adult is interfering with children interacting with one another."

RNIB was one of the first organizations to distribute Braille Bricks. Seven-year-old Laurel, from Great Yarmouth in the United Kingdom, has been learning with the tool kit. "I love using it to do my spelling homework. It's the most fun ever," she says. Her mother has also noticed that it is making learning more enjoyable for Laurel. Evie Roberts is just starting her secondary education and also has access to the bricks. "I like how they are very tactile. The surfaces are super smooth, and the dots are really clear. The dots on the bricks are bigger than the braille I usually use, but I got used to that very quickly," she says.

"Braille offers a tactile medium to access the written word," Caireen summarizes. "We would never say to a sighted child, 'You can't have access to any printed books.' And [not offering braille] would be like saying to a blind child, 'You can't have access to the printed word.' That's why braille is absolutely crucial in a child's education. It is one of many things that they should be offered in terms of their education."

LEGO Braille Bricks are now available in more than twenty countries, allowing children around the world to learn braille using the LEGO® System. The LEGO Foundation has plans to adapt this resource and make it accessible for even more users. When the LEGO brick was invented in 1958, no one imagined that it would be used as a learning tool for children with visual impairments, though its core design makes it perfectly suited to the task. LEGO Braille Bricks are yet another inspiring, innovative, and real-world application that fosters creativity, joy, and learning through play.

FACING PAGE LEGO Braille Bricks are unique because of their stud arrangements, but they are still part of the LEGO System and therefore compatible with all of the other elements.

CHAPTER 05

A Turtle in Need

THE MARYLAND ZOO'S CREATIVE LEGO® SOLUTION

The world is a treacherous place if you're an Eastern box turtle. Lawn mowers, dogs, and cars are some of the day-to-day dangers that you face while going about your turtle life. The slow-moving reptile at the heart of this story, fell victim to one of a turtle's most dangerous foes— a moving vehicle. However, with innovation, creative thinking, and a handful of LEGO® bricks, Dr. Ellen Bronson and her team at the Maryland Zoo rehabilitated this turtle and released him back into his natural habitat.

Luckily for the male turtle, his regular route was close to the Maryland Zoo in Baltimore, Maryland, and a zoo employee found him injured with a badly fractured shell. The employee took him to Dr. Ellen Bronson, the senior director of animal health, conservation, and research at the zoo. Her main responsibility is to take care of all the animals at the zoo, including the wild animals that live on the grounds.

"The Eastern box turtle is found throughout the East Coast. They used to be a very common species,"

Dr. Bronson explains. "They live in the interface between forests and water features. The area around the zoo is a watershed that goes into the Chesapeake Bay, so it is their preferred ecosystem." A wooded forest forms part of the zoo grounds, which transitions into a very large public park, giving the local Eastern box turtles a good area to make their home. Although they are a resilient species, their numbers have been declining for the last twenty years as humans encroach upon their habitats and new diseases spread in the turtle population.

These peculiar little creatures spend their lives within 250 yards of the nests they were born in. They make a mental map of the territory, so they know where to find food, and always aim to return to the same area. That means that they might cross a road to reach part of their territory, putting them at risk of being injured by traffic. "Their shell has been their ecological niche for millions of years, and they are typically very well protected—but not against a car and not against a lawn mower. If there's a really strong crushing force, it will of course harm the shell," Dr. Bronson explains. "A break in the shell is the most common trauma to a turtle of any kind. They can be fixed in rehabilitation centers, but it does take a very long time. Turtles do

THIS PAGE Dr. Bronson's team brainstormed different solutions before coming up with the idea of a LEGO wheelchair.

FACING PAGE As well as taking care of animals living within the zoo's exhibits, the Maryland Zoo looks after local wildlife nearby.

everything slowly—they have a slow metabolism—but they do heal quite well if you give them the time."

Given the local population, Dr. Bronson encounters a number of injured Eastern box turtles each year. What was unique—and particularly challenging—in this instance was that the fracture was to the bottom of the turtle's shell, which broke into seven different fragments. First, Dr. Bronson and her team needed to put the pieces together and stabilize the shell. "That already takes some ingenuity because it's basically like a broken bone, but it's external. You have to bridge all those gaps between the different fractures with different things; we used some metal bone plates that you would put into an animal or a person to stabilize the shell fragments together with glue in between. To hold the bar in place, we also used sewing hooks; we put them on either side of the fracture line and then put wire in between to pull the pieces together. We used various things for the different pieces."

It's easier to repair the top shell because it doesn't make contact with the ground, so the turtle can still move while it recovers. The turtle's bottom shell, however, is likely to make frequent contact with their terrain as they walk. For an Eastern box turtle it's even more difficult, because the species has a hinged bottom shell, also known as a plastron. The hinge offers an important form of protection, allowing the turtle to almost fully enclose itself within the shell. When it came to Dr. Bronson's task, that hinge further complicated the repair process.

Once the fragments were bridged together, there was another tricky challenge, Dr. Bronson recalls: "We needed to get the turtle off the ground, because we had all this hardware on the bottom of the turtle. But if he's doing his turtle thing

and sitting on it or dragging it along, that would harm its bottom shell." Her team considered some options. In the past they had glued different things, like half of a table tennis ball, to the bottom of turtles recovering from such fractures, to make sure the shell stayed off the ground. In this case, the multiple fractures made that impossible—there was no one piece of shell big enough to glue anything onto it. They tried making a metal structure with wheels, but that too had to be attached to the bottom of the shell.

"We had everybody on the team brainstorm what else we could do," Dr. Bronson says. Garrett Fraess, a fourth-year veterinary student, came up with the winning idea. Garrett, inspired by a friend who was a LEGO enthusiast, thought of creating a structure from LEGO bricks and attaching it to the sides of the shell. "The thinking was that there are wheels that come with LEGO kits already that attach to other LEGO elements," Dr. Bronson explains. "That would mean we didn't have to attach any wheels to the shell directly." Garrett sent the turtle's measurements to his friend so that she could build a suitable frame using LEGO elements, including some of the more complex LEGO® Technic elements to make sure it would be strong enough to withstand the reptile's movements. When it arrived at the zoo, it fit the little turtle perfectly, and the team attached it to the shell using epoxy glue that wouldn't harm the reptile.

To Dr. Bronson's delight, the turtle patient took no time at all in becoming more mobile once the contraption was fitted. "It was an immediate difference. He really didn't move much with the things that we had designed before. As soon as we put the LEGO structure on him, he immediately took off and was moving really well. It raised him up so that he could move his legs better. It was no longer painful for him to move with a bunch of fractures. He understood it immediately and started moving."

Waiting for a turtle to heal requires a lot of patience. After a couple of months of using the LEGO wheelchair, the turtle went into his brumation period—the reptile equivalent of hibernation—from October until April. During that time turtles don't do much healing, but fortunately their healing doesn't regress either. Once they awake and begin to eat and drink again, the slow healing process continues. When the zoo turtle woke up, he used the wheelchair again, before brumating for yet another winter. After two full hibernation seasons, he was well enough to be released without the LEGO aid, although some of the hardware on the shell was kept in place to help him continue to heal.

"We had to do some adjustments and multiple surgeries on [the shell]," Dr. Bronson says. "Imagine if you're a human and you have multiple broken bones—it requires multiple surgeries. Once we had the initial healing done, he was then able to use his back legs. It was really just that first year that he needed the wheelchair."

What this turtle's road to recovery illustrates is that creativity extends

FACING PAGE As soon as the turtle was fitted with the LEGO contraption, he was able to move around again independently.

To Dr. Bronson's delight, the turtle patient took no time at all in becoming more mobile once the contraption was fitted.

beyond paintings on canvases or performances on stages. It's entirely possible to bring fresh thinking to any challenge, and those out-of-the-box ideas sometimes present the best solution. "Thinking creatively is something we do every day," Dr. Bronson says. "The LEGO wheelchair was just the thing that worked the best. We use creative solutions all the time because we have so many different animals that have very unique things happen to them that we need to solve in order to take care of them medically. This creativity is something that is part of our jobs, and we're always really happy when it does work.

"There's a lot that happens at every accredited zoo behind the scenes. We hope that we inspire people to protect what's in their own backyards," Dr. Bronson says. She offers some advice for those who want to protect the wild turtles that live around them: "It's really important if you see a turtle when you're driving down the road and it is potentially in harm's way—stop, pull aside, get it off the road in the direction that it was going. You'll have saved a turtle life. If you have turtles in your backyard, create a habitat for them. Make sure they are out of the way of your lawn mower. Make sure your dogs don't get out there. They're a species that is really declining right now, and we can help in simple ways. It's a contribution that is pretty easy for individual people to make."

This turtle recovery is thanks to the team at the Maryland Zoo thinking creatively. As a result, this unique solution attracted international attention and raised awareness of wildlife conservation that can be done not only in remote and distant places, but also in our own neighborhoods and backyards.

ABOVE Turtles take a long time to heal, so it was vital that the fractured shell was raised off the ground.

CHAPTER 06

Making Micro- tonal Music

A PLAYABLE LEGO® GUITAR

Building the spirit of LEGO® creativity into a guitar is not an easy challenge. Many imaginative people have built guitars using LEGO bricks, all of which are very colorful instruments to play and display. However, most stop there—with a fantastic-looking build. Yet what makes the LEGO® System in Play so special is the way it allows for constant change and iteration, for elements to be removed and rearranged. In short, it's a medium that supports constant exploration. In the search for creative adaptations of this principle, Tolgahan Çoğulu saw the potential in innovations beyond a brick-built guitar body and neck.

Tolgahan is a professor and the founder of the classical guitar department at the Turkish Music State Conservatory, which is part of Istanbul Technical University. When Tolgahan was coming up with his version of a LEGO guitar, he was determined that it should go beyond the basics; he hoped the bricks would become integral to the experience of playing music.

Tolgahan's specialty is microtonal music, which makes use of a tuning system that is much more complex than the system usually studied in Western music classes. "A regular guitar is based on a tuning system called twelve-tone equal temperament, in which we have twelve semitones per octave," he explains. "It has been the dominant tuning system since the nineteenth century, but many music cultures—and many music genres—use more than twelve tones per octave, so these are microtones." Those micro-tones are any interval that is less than a half step (a half step, or semitone, is the interval between two adjacent notes—for example, the distance between C and C-sharp).

Although uncommon in Western music, microtones are used elsewhere around the world, including South Asia and the Middle East, as part of different musical traditions. The bağlama, tanbur, and kemençe are some of the string instruments that are often used to play the music. Tolgahan is particularly inter-ested in classical Turkish music: "Without the microtones, it's something else. The microtone is the essential brick of the traditional music." For those who are unfamiliar with microtonal music, it may sound discordant initially—some sounds are recognizable, but you hear notes you are not accustomed to, which often leads to a richer sound. To attain this range of tones, Tolgahan first conceived of a hybrid microtonal guitar that could be adjusted from one tuning system to another, and back, by adjusting the fret-board. The fretboard is what is colloquially referred to as the neck of the guitar, and the frets are the metal strips that run across it, allowing the guitarist to play different notes. Tolgahan's initial concept allowed users to change the fretboard to include the microtones they would like to play, in addition to playing the regular semitones that are found on standard guitars.

However, this already brilliant idea is naturally made better by adding LEGO elements. While Tolgahan tinkered with his guitar prototype, his seven-year-old son, Atlas Çoğulu, spent his free time playing with LEGO bricks. "I already had my adjustable microtonal guitar fretboard design with the channel slots under each string. My son was familiar with that design, so he built a copy of it using

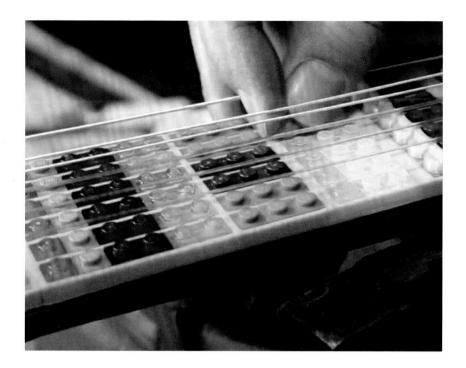

LEGO bricks. It was a really nice design, and he placed it on the standard guitar," Tolgahan says. The message from his son was clear: build this guitar out of LEGO bricks. At first, the academic dismissed the idea, as many homemade LEGO guitars had already been created. But then, he says, "We realized that nobody had tried building a fretboard, because nobody had the motivation of wanting to play microtones." That realization gave

him the impetus to run with Atlas's brick-based concept.

When Atlas built his fretboard from LEGO elements, it fit the shape of a guitar and looked the part—but the size of the bricks gave it dimensions that made the guitar unplayable. For a guitar to be functional, correct spacing of the frets is essential, especially if you want to be able to play microtones. Tolgahan enlisted the help of Ruşen Can Acet, a doctoral student in the University's Sound Engineering department, for the project. There was a lot of math involved, as the height of the frets, the placement of the strings, and the angle of the fretboard all had to be considered. With some trial and error, Ruşen 3D-printed a bespoke

ABOVE LEGO plates can be added or removed from the guitar to adjust the frets.

Adjustable frets take away the usual limitations, meaning that guitarists can play microtonal music from around the world.

fretboard with the correct spacing. The design featured standard studs that LEGO elements could fit onto.

Once the fretboard was ready, it was up to Atlas to raid his LEGO collection for the relevant elements. He dug out tiny 1×1 plates (which are one-third the height of a classic LEGO brick) to attach to the fretboard. The team then 3D-printed bespoke frets, which were compatible with LEGO bricks and could be attached to the plates.

As intended, the LEGO guitar allows someone to play different types of music that would simply not be playable on a regular guitar. Those adjustable frets take away the usual limitations, meaning that guitarists can play microtonal music from around the world—they just add the frets

that they need and remove the ones they don't. When they want to play something else, they adjust the bricks again.

Through this amazing innovation, the one-of-a-kind instrument offers a unique opportunity for teaching. Tolgahan's LEGO brick invention can be played as a regular guitar or adjusted for anything else. "Learning and teaching music theory becomes a fun proposition, especially for the kids," he says. "It becomes like playing with a toy or playing a game together."

One benefit that Tolgahan was not expecting is that the guitar can also be used to teach fretless guitar, which is a challenging instrument to learn—it takes away the frets completely to allow for a wider range of pitches. To adapt Tolgahan's instrument, it's simply a matter of removing the studded LEGO plates and replacing them with smooth LEGO tiles. Swedish online video creator Simon the

Magpie came up with the idea, which in turn also highlights the beauty of the LEGO System—people can make this guitar for themselves, modify it, share their ideas, and then see someone else take it one step further. "You inspire them, they inspire you back. It's amazing. It's a global collaboration," says Tolgahan.

The LEGO guitar was recognized in the Georgia Institute of Technology's Guthman Musical Instrument Competition, winning the People's Choice Award after going viral. Tolgahan is also overseeing a project involving the instrument a bit closer to home. "Çağatay Özkaya is a master's student in the microtonal guitar department and has a recording project playing a traditional microtonal children's tune from Turkey on the LEGO microtonal guitar." The added hook that the song is being played on a brick-enhanced instrument will help a generation unfamiliar with the traditional music discover it.

This unique project has certainly captured the music world's collective imagination. Academics, music content creators, and even bona fide rock stars have contacted Tolgahan to get their hands on their own LEGO guitar. This unique instrument explores the diversity of music across the globe, allowing people to discover something with depth and complexity using simple toy bricks. The flexibility and adaptability that this guitar offers embodies the very spirit of the LEGO System.

RIGHT The LEGO guitar can be played in different configurations—it can even be played as a fretless guitar.

CHAPTER 07

Building by Touch and Sound

MATTHEW SHIFRIN'S INCLUSIVE INSTRUCTIONS

The beauty of LEGO® building instructions is that no matter what language you speak, you can look at the image showing you what to do next and match it to the elements you have in front of you. It unites LEGO builders around the globe with a shared visual language. Designers diligently make sure each step is clearly illustrated, functional, efficient, and easily followed. But given their very nature, visual building instructions are not accessible for all. Potential builders with vision impairments cannot see the instructions, and without clear steps to follow, building a set from Bag 1 through the final brick is just out of reach.

This was Matthew Shifrin's experience. He's a lifelong LEGO fan who is legally blind. The twenty-five-year-old divides his time between attending New England Conservatory, where he is a contemporary improvisation student, and working on entrepreneurial projects that will benefit people with vision impairments.

When he was a child, he and family friend Lilya picked up a crate of loose LEGO bricks and began tinkering. Although he had played with LEGO® DUPLO® bricks when he was younger and had recently started to build LEGO® BIONICLE® action figures, this was his first experience with classic 2×4 bricks, minifigures, plates, and other elements. "I didn't have the building language [and visual cues] that a sighted kid has," he explains. "As a sighted child, you can look at box art, you can look at instructions. You can go on the LEGO website where they have alternative builds and things. I didn't have any of that information, so I would put wheels on a horse and be like, 'Hey, I made a Trojan horse.' It was cool,

but my builds weren't at the same level as my friends'. My parents would try and build with me. It would take us hours to build a small set because we'd have to go piece by piece." While Matthew's friends were building a complex X-wing starfighter or an enormous Hogwarts™ Castle, he was taking three or four hours to build a much smaller model.

Despite wanting to play with LEGO bricks, Matthew felt that he couldn't do so in the same way as his peers. His way of accessing LEGO sets was by reading reviews on shopping websites or scouring message boards for fan discussions. "Then my thirteenth birthday rolled around, and Lilya brought this giant cardboard box and a big fat binder," he says. "On the box was a braille label that read 7573 LEGO Battle of Alamut, 821 pieces.' I was very intrigued. I'd been secretly wanting that set because it had a LEGO camel."

Matthew continues, "The gift really was the binder, because in this binder were text instructions that Lilya had brailled on a braille typewriter, which is a giant, clunky, mechanical thing that has six keys on it—you punch holes in this thick, rough paper. She had created an entire language of piece names and of ways to describe the orientation of pieces vertically, horizontally, symmetrically."

Lilya learned braille to build a closer relationship with Matthew, and her ingenuity, commitment, and patience in brailling these instructions paid off, as

FACING PAGE If LEGO instructions cannot be understood visually, they must be creatively communicated in a different way, such as braille.

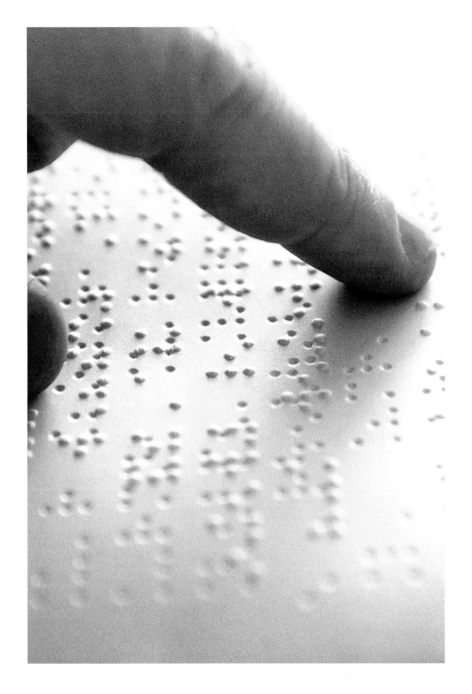

Matthew was able to complete the build independently. "It was intense," he says. "Thankfully, I was familiar with the building techniques that were used, but I spent all day building, and at the end of it, that domed castle was done. Honestly, I was riding such an emotional wave when I finished, because never in my life had I thought that I would be able to do something like this. This seemed to me like such a crucial part of childhood."

This was by no means the end of the gift, though, as Matthew and Lilya decided to share it with other people with vision impairments. Lilya wrote text-based instructions on a computer, and Matthew checked them using his braille reader, correcting anything that didn't make sense. "We wanted to give this incredible experience to other blind kids. I was in an extremely privileged situation—I had a friend who was so creative that she adapted things for me." Not everyone had a Lilya in their life, so it became Matthew's mission to pay his friend's kindness and generosity forward.

The pair started a website where they shared the text-based instructions

"LEGO models are also really valuable from a fictional standpoint. When blind people watch movies or television, there's a narrator in the background telling them what's happening. The trouble is, the narrator doesn't really have the time to talk about the scenery or what a vehicle looks like. I went to the LEGO headquarters in Billund, Denmark, and they had the *Millennium Falcon* on display. I said, 'Wow, I didn't know the *Millennium Falcon* looked like a depressed pancake.' You know it's Han Solo's spaceship, but you really have no idea what it entails."

The most complex LEGO sets tend to be part of the LEGO® Technic theme, which focuses on engineering and constructing working vehicles. "In fourth grade, we had science class; we were talking about simple machines, levers, and pulleys, and all that stuff," Matthew says. "My friends were building these LEGO sets, and you could build a pulley that would lift a minifigure up. I was in awe. Even though LEGO Technic is more abstract, it's really valuable to adapt those types of sets as well; whatever engineering concept you'd like to convey [to someone with a vision impairment] has probably already been discussed in a LEGO set. Even though it is more of a brain strain for a blind person, it's still crucial to try and learn as much from the medium as you can."

with other LEGO users. They had a great response, with parents contacting them with requests for specific set instructions and other people just getting in touch with supportive messages. The outpouring of joy drove the pair's passion to expand. Many of the sets that they provided instructions for were chosen because they represented real locations. For a person with a vision impairment, these models can be a way to understand the world. "I can't climb a building—I'm not Spider-Man," Matthew says with a laugh. "When you build landmarks like the Tower Bridge or the Statue of Liberty out of LEGO bricks as a blind person, you're able to really engage with the parts of the world that are untouchable to you.

Several months after building that first set with text-based instructions, Matthew's life was turned upside down. "Lilya was diagnosed with stage 4 cancer," Matthew recalls. "It was very hard—you wanted to melt into a depressed puddle. But you couldn't do that. She was not melting into a depressed puddle. She was really taking

ABOVE A braille typewriter similar to the one Lilya used for Matt's domed castle instructions.

FACING PAGE Matthew with his collection of LEGO modular buildings.

things as they came. It was incredible, because she'd come home from chemo, I'd call her, and she would have no energy to talk—yet she was still writing instructions. She had a sorting process where she took the bricks for each step of a set, and she'd sort them into separate bags and label them in braille so I could build faster and wouldn't have to slog through piles of parts. And she still did that. It was incredible."

Despite a prognosis of having less than a year to live, Lilya lived for five more years. "She was translating books from Russian to English," Matthew admired. "She was tutoring children on the autism spectrum. She was going to church every Sunday, living such a full and engaging life. During that time, she adapted forty LEGO sets." After Lilya's death, Matthew wanted to keep creating instructions to share on their website but didn't know how without Lilya's help. It wasn't something he could do by himself; he needed some assistance. He reached out to the LEGO Group and eventually found himself speaking to Olaf Gjerlufsen of the LEGO Creative Play Lab.

The conversations went well. "It turned out that the LEGO Group had text-based

ABOVE LEGO models of famous landmarks allow people with visual impairments to experience them through touch.

"When you build landmarks like the Tower Bridge or the Statue of Liberty out of LEGO bricks as a blind person, you're able to really engage with the parts of the world that are untouchable to you."

instructions built into their system, in the sense that the language that they use for making LEGO instructions has text-based elements in it," Matthew explains. "He needed to find programmers who could take this text-based information and turn it into instructions that could easily be comprehended by you, me, or whomever. He found people from the Austrian Institute of Technology, and they created this algorithm that would use artificial intelligence to take graphical instructions and then convert them to text-based ones."

This artificial intelligence workflow cut out the time-consuming process of someone sitting down to write the instructions for each stage of a set. Four LEGO sets were trialed for the initial pilot of LEGO® Audio & Braille Instructions to see whether they worked for people with vision impairments. Available to everyone online, these instructions could be accessed by audio track, screen reader, or braille reader. By the end of 2021, the LEGO Group made audio instructions for forty-five different sets available, including a set from LEGO Technic. "As soon as

instructions are ready, I make sure that they are buildable by blind people before release. There are small errors, like in any instructions, so it's just about correcting and clarifying them," says Matthew. "I'm just so glad that these instructions are able to bring joy to other people, the same kind of joy that I got when I built that [first] set. And I'm glad that Lilya's method is as valid and understandable to others as it is to me."

Lilya Finkel's creation and inspiration live on through the LEGO Audio & Braille Building Instruction program. Her dedication to creating instructions for Matthew now provides joy and play for LEGO builders with vision impairments around the world, demonstrating that the tenacity, creativity, and commitment of one young person can change the world.

ABOVE LEGO Audio & Braille Instructions allow children with visual impairments to build a model, step by step.

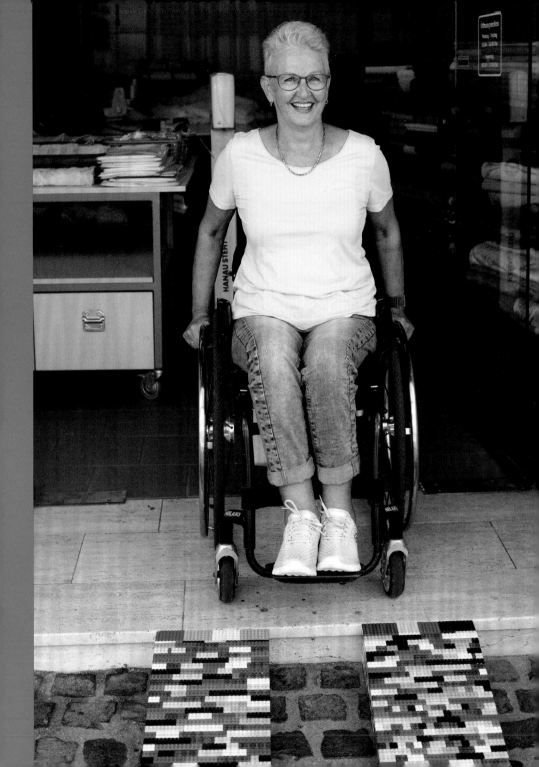

CHAPTER 08

Ramps with Color

A BRICK-BUILT SOLUTION FOR WHEELCHAIR USERS

Rita Ebel of Hanau, Germany, regularly encounters a situation other wheelchair users are also all too familiar with: She is outside a store that she would like to enter, but she is not able to go in because there is no wheelchair access. Merely one step or an elevated door threshold has the potential to derail a quick errand or visit to a local business. However, Rita came across a creative solution she was determined to put into practice: to build wheelchair ramps using LEGO® bricks so that wheelchair users could access the same places as people not living with disabilities.

Despite decades of advocacy and activism inspired by the global disability rights movement, wheelchair accessibility is still not fully realized. Rita knew exactly how she could help herself and others, and she was committed to making it happen. Her new mission was inspired by a news report she saw about an individual who built LEGO wheelchair ramps in Bielefeld, Germany, three hours north of Hanau. The idea for these brick ramps did not originate in Bielefeld, but instead it passed by word of mouth, and now the concept's origins are untraceable. No one cares to claim ownership of the idea because these brick builders just want to make a positive change by increasing accessibility for all.

The LEGO brick ramps are constructed from classic two-stud-wide bricks. This construction provides enough stability for a wheelchair to make it through a doorway because of how strong the elements are when clicked together. The LEGO stud and tube coupling system paired with the ability to adapt the height by stacking multiple bricks made LEGO

ABOVE Colorful LEGO ramps have become a tourist attraction in Hanau, Germany.

elements the perfect material for varying ramp elevations and differing terrain. Some of the ramps come in a set of two, each one relatively thin so that they can be spaced to create a track for two wheels of a wheelchair. Others are one solid block that fit the entire width of the doorway. As a bonus, with the rainbow of bricks available, the ramps give a colorful flair to the shop entrances where they are placed.

Once Rita set her mind to building a LEGO wheelchair ramp, she quickly realized she would need a lot of LEGO bricks. "It's astounding how many treasures are lying around in people's basements or attics, where the grandchildren are too old to play with them, but they're too good to be thrown away. Every time there was

ABOVE Rita and the volunteers build fun designs into their ramps.

any kind of city event, I would sit at the marketplace and ask for donations. But wow—it went really, really slowly," Rita explains.

Undeterred, she decided to build mini ramps to demonstrate the ultimate goal. The models went on display in local stores with flyers and posters, encouraging people to donate their unwanted LEGO elements. It took a while, but bricks started trickling in. Rita's persistence paid off when someone selling loose LEGO elements online reached out to her to ask how many bricks she needed to finish the first ramp. He sent two boxes of bricks, free of charge.

With the donation in hand, though, Rita still had yet another hurdle to overcome. "I went through Hanau and talked to different stores, and they didn't want [a ramp]," she says. But then, luckily, an acquaintance of Rita's, who is also a wheelchair user, told her a story about going into a shop but not being able to get back out again. This gave Rita the tip she needed to find the right store to feature her inaugural LEGO ramp. "There was a young employee who was very excited and told me she'd convince her boss that they needed something like this." Sure enough, the owner agreed, and Rita's first ramp was installed.

Getting the initial ramp in place was important so other businesses could see the concept in action. While word of Rita's ramps spread naturally from store to store, her tenacity and savvy marketing also helped as she invited the press

to see the first installation. Before long, many shops and businesses in Hanau had colorful LEGO wheelchair ramps in their entryways. Some were just built with attractive patterns, while others had the business logo designed into them. Tourists started seeking out Rita's ramps to pose for photos and post on social media.

On a municipal level, one of the difficulties with making places wheelchair accessible is that there are regulations about the size of ramps and their gradient. The regulations can lead to situations where those requirements prevent permanent ramps from being installed, such as when there isn't enough space on the sidewalk to install one. However, because the LEGO ramps are easily moved and are not fixed in place, they offer a flexible solution that shop owners quickly learned could better serve their customers.

With the project's growing renown, sourcing LEGO bricks was no longer a problem. "I get packages of LEGO bricks in the mail from people, and there are always really kind letters enclosed, saying how great they think the idea is and how nice it is. Through their donation, they're now involved in the project themselves," Rita explains. In the early days, Rita would ask specifically for classic two-stud-wide LEGO bricks, but she realized that potential donors didn't necessarily have time to sort their elements before donating them. She now trades the more specialized elements for rectangular two-stud-wide bricks from LEGO merchants who support her work.

The message has spread far beyond Hanau, and even Germany. Rita is in touch with people around the world who want to make a difference in their community, including people from Austria, Switzerland, Italy, and Russia. Some of these fellow builders create the ramps themselves using instructions that Rita has designed and shares freely online, while others enlist her to build a ramp for them. It's not just a case of passing over the building guide, though. She also provides guidance on cultivating community support. When she is building a ramp and sending it overseas, she also talks through the whole process, making sure her participants understand how to determine the height of the ramp and the type of ground surface necessary to support it. When spreading her message, Rita is clear that someone else should be present when the ramp is in use for the safety of the wheelchair user.

Rita believes that nondisabled people are simply not aware of concerns of accessibility that people living with physical disabilities must often consider. "For many people, when they don't have experience with [a disability], it's just unconscious. There's no bad intention, they just don't know this problem," she says. Her project is increasing the awareness of all citizens in participating communities. "People are thinking much more about accessibility because, through the colorful ramps, something loosens in their minds and people begin thinking about the story. That's just as important a result as someone being able to enter a store that they weren't able to enter before." She expands, "People are becoming attentive. Before the ramps they would just walk past such a step, and now, suddenly, they say, 'I never noticed this step before.' People become aware of how many steps there are and how problematic that is: It's

not just wheelchair users, but also people using walkers, or parents with strollers."

Thanks to her hard work, Rita is known by many as the LEGO *Oma*, a nickname coined by her granddaughter that translates to "LEGO Grandma." Now, Rita has a team of eight volunteers who support the project. Globally, they have built more than seventy-five ramps in just three years and have shared building instructions more than six hundred times. As for Rita, she now finds much of her time taken up by sharing her story and responding to messages from all over the world. She even visits schools to talk to the children about wheelchair ramps and accessibility.

It's quite remarkable that a small-scale project in a German city has spread around the world and inspired countless people to make thoughtful changes in their own communities, demonstrating how a simple idea can have an unexpectedly outsized impact.

"For many people, when they don't have experience with [a disability], it's just unconscious. There's no bad intention, they just don't know this problem."

CHAPTER 09

Art for All

JEFF FRIESEN'S LEGO® APPROACH TO STREET ART

Street art, which is so often covered over within days of its creation, is similar to a LEGO® build—once you complete something in bricks, it is ready to be pulled down again so those elements can be reused for a new creation. These are two vastly different forms of creativity that share a temporary state as well as an incredible opportunity for play. When professional photographer Jeff Friesen discovered that modern storytelling with LEGO bricks and minifigures complemented the aesthetic of Banksy, the legendary street artist, he decided to embark on an ambitious project to reimagine works from the world's most famous (and anonymous) artist using the world's most popular toy.

Starting in the 1990s, Banksy confounded the art world with his creative body of work found across the streets of Bristol, England. To this day, in the cover of night, the secretive artist uses empty building exteriors and public walls as his canvas. In the morning, the public sees his witty, often humorous, and always subversive art stenciled across the streets. His subject matter, his guerrilla-style process, and the mystery that shrouds his identity contributes to Banksy's ongoing critique of institutions and the commodification of art. However, despite Banksy's intention to avoid in the buying and selling of his own art, his name is now world-famous, and his art is often removed (along with the wall it was painted on) and sold to the highest bidder.

Had Banksy not gained this global notoriety, the chances are high that his stenciled images would be painted over as quickly as the taking apart of a LEGO build. Perhaps that's why Jeff's playfully named *Bricksy* images became a viral sensation around the world.

The Canadian photographer had LEGO elements as a child—he remembers playing with 2×4 and 2×8 bricks in red and white. It wasn't until his daughter was born, though, that he started interacting with LEGO elements as an adult. "I was always interested in LEGO products," he explains. "I would shuffle off to the toy section of any store I was in. Then my daughter was born in 2006, and as soon as she was old enough, she had every LEGO set. We would just spend hours. I was making very elaborate things like tiny worlds in microscale. She would actually play with them and use little 1×1 round plates as people."

Jeff saw the potential for photographing LEGO models thanks to minifigures, the little figurines that inhabit the LEGO System. When minifigures arrived in 1978, they all had the same expression, and there were only a couple of hairpieces to choose from. All that changed in 2010 with the introduction of a new product range that caught Jeff's eye: the Collectible LEGO® Minifigures Series. The widely popular Collectible Minifigures Series mystery pack contains elements that, when assembled, are little characters with specific bios and identities. For example, there might be a girl in a bee costume or a sci-fi repair robot or even a knight from medieval times; collectors never know which minifigure they are going to receive.

The variety of minifigure elements after 2010—with new wigs, expressions, and body parts—allowed Jeff to mix and match his minifigure characters more freely than ever before. "All of a sudden,

there was a variety of minifigures; there were lots of people to choose from," he says. "I'm from Victoria, this really cold city in Canada where everybody's still a headbanger—we listen to heavy metal; we have long hair and mustaches and drive muscle cars. I made a funny picture of this headbanger guy with his hot rod car in the snow and his girlfriend pushing him out. Then I made a stereotypical scene for every province in Canada."

After playing around with regional personalities in his own country, Jeff then made a scene for every state in the United States. Following his brick tour of North America, the Canadian turned his attention across the pond, building London scenes with quintessential British characteristics. Immersion in the United Kingdom led Jeff to re-create a Banksy piece. He explains, "Street art and LEGO bricks are seemingly opposing things, but they're both giant pop culture phenomena. Street art is so gritty, yet LEGO bricks are so modern, clean, and largely known as a child's toy." The idea of creating a series of Banksy pieces with LEGO elements really excited Jeff. "I could hardly sleep, and then after a month of making them I put them online. They went viral. It was all pretty crazy. Banksy even had them on his own Instagram."

ABOVE Jeff's first LEGO photograph was a tribute to his home city of Victoria, Canada.

Jeff has a few favorites, one of which is a classic Banksy image that everyone knows well. "Balloon Girl is the most universally loved of all of Banksy's works, since its message of hope resonates with everyone," he says. "The LEGO version continues the same meaning. I made the background buildings drab and shabby to contrast with the bright minifigure girl and the oversized red balloon. It's a visual reference to the Oscar Wilde quote: 'We are all in the gutter, but some of us are looking at the stars.'"

Rats feature often in Banksy's imagery. Some say the animal represents the never-ending presence of street art—people try to remove it but to no end, because if one piece is removed then three more appear in its place, much like a rat that continues to prevail despite its unfortunate reputation. Jeff wanted to create something featuring an iconic Banksy subject. He envisioned the rat to be walking a tightrope—and the two-stud-long LEGO rat element wouldn't do the job. "Having the LEGO brick–built rat be capable of holding objects meant it had to be about fifteen feet tall in minifigure scale. I wasn't a skilled LEGO builder at the time, so the big rat went through many iterations. The necessarily large scale has the fun side effect of bringing rats out of the shadows and onto the center stage. It's a visual reference to Banksy making rats famous," Jeff says.

Over the years, many adults like Jeff have found new ways of creating with LEGO bricks, demonstrating that just as they are perfect for children's play, they can also be used by adults in interesting and artistic ways. For Jeff, there is inherent humor in LEGO minifigures, which is why they seem to lend themselves so well to the clever and witty Banksy pieces. Each of Jeff's images reimagines one of Banksy's classic murals. Some of them are very straightforward LEGO brick representations of the original artwork, and others add a twist. For example, Banksy's original *Keep It Real* features a gorilla with a sandwich board, while the *Bricksy* version places the ape on the London Underground, with other characters looking at it.

The process for making each *Bricksy* image was very basic, with the minifigures front and center. "I just used a pile of bricks to make the background buildings, then the ground I made with construction paper. Sometimes the sky was also construction paper," Jeff explains. By

ABOVE "Laugh now, but one day we'll be in charge," reads one of Banksy's most recognizable images.

ABOVE The Gorilla Suit Guy minifigure is placed in various settings, with subtle twists on the billboard adjusting the meaning.

ABOVE The simple and stark imagery of Banksy's famous work is captured using LEGO bricks.

keeping the backdrops simple, he ensured that nothing detracts from the focal point of the images. The photographs usually took at least as long as actually building the scene and setting it up with the characters. "It was all combined in a pretty simple tabletop studio setup. I'm a bit of a perfectionist, so I would take fifty or sixty versions of each one."

The entire project came about through Jeff's appreciation of Banksy's imagery. "In the realm of street art, there really aren't that many famous artists, but somehow Banksy became really famous. I got into Banksy after I saw his movie, *Exit through the Gift Shop*. This guy is some kind of a genius, mocking the whole art world," Jeff says.

Given that Jeff continues to work with his collection of LEGO bricks since creating the *Bricksy* scenes, he has probably demolished countless numbers of his own creations—beating Banksy to the punch.

In 2018 Banksy publicly shredded a piece of his art using a specially designed frame right after it sold at auction for $1.4 million. As long as the secretive artist keeps surprising and subverting with his work, he will continue to inspire Jeff and other creatives to do the very same.

ABOVE Rats are a common theme in Banksy's body of work.

CHAPTER 10

Play Included

HOW LEGO® BRICKS HELP NEURODIVERGENT CHILDREN

When presented with a pile of LEGO® bricks, every child will build something different because everyone is wired just a little bit differently. Whether they are following instructions or creating something new from their own imaginations, the LEGO® System in Play encourages all children, wherever they are and however they experience the world, to explore their own boundless creativity. The benefits of play are limitless—children may discover special skills and interests; or learn how to make friends; or solve problems. With such vast opportunities to learn and develop, LEGO play is a powerful tool for neurodivergent children to experiment, adapt, and grow.

Founded and directed by Dr. Gina Gómez de la Cuesta and Dr. Elinor Brett, Play Included is a social enterprise that applies the power of play to help children make sense of the world. It is the leading resource in the Brick-by-Brick® program—a child-led, learning through play concept using LEGO bricks. Thanks to the team there, autistic and other neurodivergent children with an interest in LEGO bricks can go to Brick Club (which is what children know the Brick-by-Brick program as) to find opportunities for socializing and interaction in a safe and supportive environment.

Dr. Gómez de la Cuesta is a registered clinical psychologist whose interest in supporting autistic people developed when she was in high school. She volunteered for a summer camp for neurodivergent children and spent time with a seventeen-year-old autistic girl, eventually developing a friendship. "We both liked singing, so we just sang together. It was really, really nice,"

Dr. Gómez de la Cuesta recalls. She continued her education and trained to be a teacher before becoming interested in psychology. Combining psychology with her interest in autism, she completed her PhD at the University of Cambridge's Autism Research Centre. Her research focused on how LEGO bricks and building activities can be used to support autistic children in their social and emotional development. Her research brought her into contact with Dr. Daniel LeGoff, who had pioneered the therapeutic benefits of LEGO bricks in the United States.

"Each autistic person has their own strengths and challenges they face. It's really important to get to know the individual person," Dr. Gómez de la Cuesta says. "Generally, neurodivergent children may view the world and experience the world in a different way [to how most other people view the world]. They are often treated differently by society. Perhaps because they are misunderstood, they are often excluded from social opportunities." Society's othering of neurodivergent people, or the conscious and subconscious practice of making neurodivergent people feel different and excluded, is very significant in the approach that Dr. Gómez de la Cuesta and her team at Play Included employ.

In the past, academic discussions about autistic people were often deficit-focused; research highlighted the things an individual was perceived to be lacking rather than looking at the whole person. In many cases, differences were perceived as weaknesses only because the world is set up to value other traits or skills. More recently, autistic adults campaigned for change, wanting to be listened to and understood rather than "fixed" of the qualities that make up who they are. "To reduce stigma and support autistic people, a lot more needs to be done to increase acceptance and understanding of different ways of thinking, communicating, and experiencing the world," says Dr. Gómez de la Cuesta. "With the right support in place and with the right understanding, autistic people can really thrive. It's a two-way street. It's not about trying to change the person's autism or change their identity. It's about giving them the opportunity to build friendships and have relationships in a way that is manageable for them."

The Brick-by-Brick program is designed to give neurodivergent children opportunities to flourish. "We're trying to value autistic play, using the flow that children and adults often get into when they're playing and building with LEGO models. We're trying to do that in a way that children can socialize together and feel part of the group, so they have a sense of belonging and social identity in their play," Dr. Gómez de la Cuesta explains. Rather than having a specific lesson plan or desired educational outcomes, Brick Club is purely about allowing neurodivergent children to get involved in playful LEGO activities. By doing so, they naturally strengthen different skills, make new friends, and become more confident.

The way the sessions are set up varies, so children are not playing in the same way each time. Sometimes they might build in a trio with distinct roles; sometimes they might build with an

ABOVE The Brick-by-Brick program provides a safe and supportive environment for neurodivergent children to interact.

"Each autistic person has their own strengths and challenges they face. It's really important to get to know the individual person."

PLAY INCLUDED | 93

adult; sometimes they might free-build a single model as a group. Older children can even make stop-motion movies, with each child taking on a specific part of the process.

Socializing and making new friends are two of the biggest benefits that Brick Club provides. "Sometimes in my groups, kids came from different schools to a clinic, and often it was the first time they'd met someone else with an autism diagnosis. They might not have known they had an autism diagnosis, but kids can tell when they're similar to each other," Dr. Gómez de la Cuesta says. Being around other children with an

activity as the focal point can make interactions easier than they would be in a free-play environment, such as a school lunch break.

The Brick-by-Brick program has led to many rewarding moments for Dr. Gómez de la Cuesta, with one in particular sticking in her mind: "One of the children says it's a place where he doesn't feel stressed and he can be himself, that he's learned what friendship means. It enabled him to feel more confident at school outside of Brick Club. Sadly, we see too many autistic children being bullied and not treated with the respect that they deserve. Brick Club gave him this insight to say, 'Actually, that's not OK.' It's been very powerful for him and for his mental health."

"Brick Club has helped me to learn how to talk to people and not be afraid

ABOVE The Brick-by-Brick program allows children to meet and socialize through a common interest in LEGO building.

to speak out loud in a group," says Ben, a Brick Club attendee, enthusiastically sharing the benefits of the club. "I have made new friends at Brick Club, and by learning how to join in conversations, I have found it easier to talk to kids at school, go by myself to ask questions at shops, and go on the bus with a friend without being anxious."

Play Included trains professionals in the Brick-by-Brick program, allowing teachers to start their own Brick Clubs and offer this service to even more neurodivergent children. One of the key things that the facilitators are taught is that the experience should be child-led. Dr. Gómez de la Cuesta shares, "There's some structure and we're trying to get everybody to collaborate, build together, and take turns, but the adult should be playfully facilitating, rather than telling children what to do or the right way to do it."

In 2021 the LEGO Foundation—the corporate foundation that owns 25 percent of the LEGO Group—partnered with Play Included. The LEGO Foundation is committed to promoting and helping deliver play for children in ways that reimagine learning. With this well-established and well-funded support, Play Included can now deliver training to more educators around the world. "We want to be a hub where people can find out accurate information, get best practice ideas, get resources, and be curious about what works," says Dr. Gómez de la Cuesta. Play Included is looking beyond educators to also develop resources for families to support children when they're at home. With LEGO building being such a beloved family activity, it's easy to see

how specialist resources could unlock new ways to play for families with neurodivergent members.

Since Dr. Gómez de la Cuesta completed her PhD and founded this social enterprise, Play Included and the Brick-by-Brick program surpassed its initial focus on autistic children, leading her to work with a broader range of neurodivergent children. The resources have continued to develop, with input from autistic adults and the LEGO Foundation helping to shape the programs. "Autistic people have loads of strengths, like being really brilliantly focused on something of interest. Or they might view the world from a different perspective. That makes you think, question, and see the world differently," says Dr. Gómez de la Cuesta.

ABOVE Dr. Gómez de la Cuesta is dedicated to bringing LEGO play to all neurodivergent kids.

CHAPTER 11

Re-
storing
Coral
Reefs

RESEARCH FOR THE FUTURE

Reefs are often celebrated for their beauty, but they are much more than that: They are unique natural environments critical to all living things, both on land and at sea. Although reefs cover only 0.2 percent of the seafloor, they support more than 25 percent of marine life. Tiny corals—invertebrate animals made up of calcium carbonate—form reefs in warm, shallow seas. Despite being microscopic individually, they are the building blocks of the reef and, much like LEGO® bricks, they become something even greater when they are combined.

Tragically, corals and the thousands of other species that inhabit reefs are under threat from a variety of humanmade factors. The Tropical Marine Science Institute (TMSI) of the National University of Singapore, however, is dedicated to bringing scientists from different disciplines together to work on restoration projects related to the ocean and marine life—and

LEGO bricks are one of the tools they use to do their work.

Corals are colonial organisms that have a symbiotic relationship with photosynthetic microalgae that sustain marine life. As primary producers at the base of the food chain, corals support the reef ecosystem's complex food webs. "These corals produce calcium carbonate skeletons as they grow, and with time and under the right conditions, they become massive three-dimensional structures that form the framework to support other marine life in coral reef habitats," says senior research fellow Dr. Jani Thuaibah Isa Tanzil. In short, corals are the most basic building blocks of their ecosystem. Without them, thousands of other species would not survive.

Regrettably, rising water temperatures and the impact of human activity have led to significant damage to coral reefs. Coral mining (where explosives are used to break up coral reefs and the segments are then taken to be sold), pollution, warming oceans, and reduced water quality are just a few of the causes of coral reef degradation. The more human activity that takes place, the greater the impact on coral reefs. Maintaining and restoring the reef is an urgent challenge; the longer they degrade, the harder it will be to conserve what remains.

Reefs around the southern islands of Singapore are an important source of biodiversity, with almost one-third of the world's total coral species recorded in this particular area. Similar to other areas around the world, Singapore's reefs have decreased in size from more than 19 square miles (50 square kilometers) to just 5 square miles (13 square kilometers)

ABOVE LEGO bricks are built into custom structures to grow coral in the lab.

ABOVE LEGO bricks provide a framework for the corals.

ABOVE Different coral species growing on LEGO elements in the lab.

after fifty years of coastal development. Underwater visibility has dropped from more than 32 feet (10 meters) in the 1960s to around 6.5 feet (2 meters) today—an extreme reduction due to water pollution. These numbers demonstrate the devastation the reefs are experiencing. "Despite these numerous environmental challenges, corals in Singapore still exhibit high species diversity and high coral growth rates when compared to neighboring reefs within the region," says Dr. Tanzil optimistically.

Given the corals' precarious situation, the researchers at the TMSI are attempting to culture more resilient corals and other reef marine life such as giant clams, cowries, and seagrass in a lab environment.

"Our current project is not only trying to find solutions that will allow us to scale up coral culture in Singapore, but also other important threatened reef organisms," says Dr. Tanzil. "I see the work we do as a small puzzle piece in the larger seascape of past and ongoing efforts in Singapore. It's continuing decades of other coral research and reef restoration projects. For countries like Singapore, where we do not have enough reefs left to transplant corals from one 'healthy' reef to another degraded reef, finding a way to sustainably produce coral stocks [in a lab] is key."

Research assistant Wei Long Ow Yong is also working on the problem. "I focus on investigating methods for culturing corals in the aquarium setting. We are aiming to upscale coral culture in a lab setting for research, as well as culture corals together with other marine organisms to explore the interactions and relationships between them. As such, we aim to find out the ideal conditions to grow the corals in," he says.

Vertical farming has been used to grow increased amounts of food in a smaller footprint on land; by growing taller plants, farmers can get a greater crop yield in a smaller space. LEGO bricks allow the research team to try this method with corals in their lab. As Dr. Tanzil notes, using LEGO elements in scientific experiments isn't a novel idea: "Coral scientists have been using LEGO bricks for experimental setups for quite some time, and it's something we have used for several years prior to this project. Having said that, the use of LEGO bricks for culturing corals in an aquarium setting like this is something new. This really started out as just an idea in passing but was taken up as a serious challenge by Wei Long, who really has been the one to make it work with his boundless creativity. The way LEGO bricks work make it easy, because the building blocks can be configured—and reconfigured—in a multitude of ways and used many times over. Just to be clear, we are only using the LEGO bricks in our lab [for culturing purposes] and not putting them out at sea."

The practicalities of the project first involve collecting loose coral fragments from the reef, then breaking them up and attaching them to traditional LEGO bricks. If done correctly, breaking coral will not do much harm to the organisms. Most corals exist as colonies, made up of

TOP The marine life cultured vertically.

BOTTOM Close-up of a broken coral polyp attached to a LEGO brick.

a whole bunch of individual clones of the coral animals, or polyps. When properly fragmented, these groups of polyps can repopulate and grow into larger individual colonies. After the polyps are broken and attached to the LEGO bricks without harm using marine epoxy, they are left to grow. LEGO bricks are the support structure of choice because they allow for a modular system. Once the coral fragments in the lab grow in size, they are propagated to produce more corals that continue to grow, providing a sustainable supply of corals for research. Eventually, the research will inform reef restoration projects conducted outside the lab in the waters surrounding Singapore.

Wei Long explains the origin of the method: "The idea of using LEGO bricks came about when Dr. Tanzil wanted to attach corals onto something stable but easily movable at the same time. She showed me how other marine scientists have used LEGO bricks in their experimental work. Initially, we had used LEGO bricks as simple stands for our coral fragments, but since they are so versatile, I thought, 'Why stop there?'" We began using them to create a variety of structures to cater to our research needs. In addition to the vertical coral culture setup, I have also used LEGO elements to create partitions and more complex coral holders."

It's not just the LEGO® System that proves useful for scientific experiments. Flooring tiles, golf tees, pegs, cement blocks, and pipes are just some of the other common objects used to culture corals in the research lab. LEGO bricks, however, offer a unique potential, unlike some of the other unconventional lab equipment. Dr. Tanzil explains, "It's modular, scalable, reusable, and secure enough that the bricks attach to one another yet can also be easily taken apart." Also, Wei Ling adds, "They are user-friendly. LEGO bricks do not require much explanation to teach new students and other researchers how to use them, as most of us have grown up with LEGO bricks as part of our childhoods. I am excited to explore new ways that LEGO elements can help us in our scientific work."

Based on the lab research done using these LEGO brick coral cultures, Dr. Tanzil and Wei Ling continue to study these complex organisms in the hopes that they might help save Singapore's reefs from extinction. The ingenuity of projects like this one demonstrates scientists' determination to come up with inventive ways to support the natural world. Fresh thinking and new approaches will be needed if unique ecosystems are going to be maintained in the face of continued human interference. While the problems are complex, sometimes the solutions do not require high-tech equipment or expensive new tools. Sometimes it's about using a simple brick that is at hand.

"Initially, we had used LEGO bricks as simple stands for our coral fragments, but since they are so versatile, I thought, 'Why stop there?'"

CHAPTER 12

Seniors Who Build

HOW KITTY SHORT REACHES PEOPLE IN NEED

Sometimes, you are knocked back a few times before you are able to execute a great idea. Not everyone can see a vision as clearly as the person who conceived it—others may need to be convinced of its worth. Kitty Short was certain that bringing LEGO® bricks into nursing homes could benefit the residents, but it took a lot of persistence before she succeeded in her mission.

Many nursing and retirement facilities face challenges finding age-appropriate activities, and it can be expensive to arrange sessions and services. Despite those barriers, it is vital that seniors are given meaningful social and leisure activities, as this type of interaction boosts their quality of life and well-being. Particularly for residents with dementia, participation in activities is mentally stimulating, and social opportunities have been shown to have mental health benefits.

That's where LEGO bricks and building come in. Kitty Short, a former drama teacher, previously worked with children to build their confidence through brick-based activities and other creative pursuits in schools. Building with LEGO bricks can benefit children, as it allows them to participate in an engaging activity to explore new ideas and problem-solving in a playful way. Similar benefits are often associated with the effects of a mindfulness practice.

Given that children enjoyed these benefits, it occurred to Kitty that there was the potential for bringing LEGO bricks to seniors in retirement homes and using similar methods to those she used when working with young people. Unfortunately, her idea was quite unusual for the nursing homes she initially approached. "I asked them, 'Would you like to try it?' They said, 'No, thank you very much.' I was feeling quite deflated," Kitty recalls. She was certain, though, that her concept would work and that seniors would benefit from it, so she didn't give up.

She decided she needed to look beyond traditional retirement homes. A local supermarket had a community room where different groups could meet up, so she tried to introduce a LEGO activity with a seniors' group. The response was less than positive; the group members dismissed the LEGO® System as a children's toy. "One lady could probably see that I looked like I was desperate and said, 'I'll have a go.' We made a little LEGO sheep, and she was lovely," Kitty says. This was the small victory Kitty needed. She achieved her goal to have a small group

ABOVE Kitty Short brings LEGO building activities to seniors and people with dementia.

"It probably took about four or five sessions until I actually thought it was working, that LEGO building with seniors actually does work and can be used."

building models collaboratively, even if it was just her and a sympathetic friend.

Kitty kept pursuing the project and found a nursing home that was happy to have her visit, where she could facilitate the seniors building as a team. "It probably took about four or five sessions until I actually thought it was working, that LEGO building with seniors actually does work and can be used. It was a really lovely moment when it clicked," she says.

This is how Kitty's collaborative building typically works: Each group of three seniors starts with a pile of LEGO bricks and an instruction book that shows how to build the model step-by-step. "You have an instructor; that's the person who reads the instructions," she says. "Then you've got the searcher; that's the person who is looking for the pieces. And then you've got the builder. You make sure they're all really clear on the roles. Sometimes I show them the finished model, so

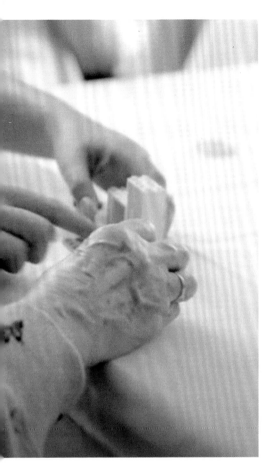

because some people will be at different levels of dementia. Perseverance because, like anything, it's difficult at first."

Kitty reminds the participants that they don't have to complete the model, but she frequently stays later than scheduled when the groups are eager to make sure their build is finished. Sets that might take a younger person fifteen minutes to build can sometimes take an hour for seniors or individuals living with dementia. Seniors might not have the dexterity in their fingers they once did. Kitty provides magnifying glasses in case participants need to zoom in on the tiny LEGO elements in the instruction books or LEGO piles. It's little touches like this that make the activity suitable for this specific age group.

Everything about the process is geared toward engaging seniors. The instructor finds ways to describe the elements and what must be done with them; the searcher interprets the description and understanding which element it refers to; the builder pays attention to where it must be placed and getting the tactile sensation of attaching it. This collaborative building becomes a social activity, encouraging communication as part of a shared experience.

"They say things like, 'I feel like my senses have been awoken,' which is very nice to hear. They just really engage with it. It's interactive, it's stimulating, and it's something that they probably wouldn't normally do. Having ownership of something gives them that little sense of achievement," Kitty says.

In Kitty's role, flexibility is absolutely vital. Everyone she meets is different, and it's important that she can improvise when

they can actually see it in the flesh. From there they just start building."

Kitty offers thoughtful advice. "I always say there are three Ps—patience, perseverance, and personality. You've got to bring the best out of their personalities. Remind everyone to be patient

ABOVE Kitty helping a senior builder click together a couple bricks.

necessary. One of the homes where she facilitated build sessions had three particular residents who didn't get along—and while she didn't manage to get the three of them to be friends, she could get them to build LEGO sets together. Through the activity, they found common ground, such as having husbands who had worked as engineers. Kitty's introduction to LEGO building helped improve their relationships beyond the social activity. Some senior residents have adopted building with LEGO bricks outside her visits, renewing a childhood pastime decades after they left it behind. "There is a guy, John, who was obsessed with LEGO bricks. He was making stuff as soon as I'd left the building," Kitty says. The activity reminded him of building LEGO sets with white houses and red roofs when he was young.

Particularly for an older generation, there can be a stigma about playing with something that is designed for children. "There was one gentleman who had a stroke," Kitty recalls. "It took me about three tries to persuade him to try it; he thought it was patronizing. Once he'd had a go, though, he loved it."

Kitty has also used LEGO bricks to build bridges between different generations. She organized a group called Brick Based Buddies, which connected autistic children with seniors. Each child was paired up with a senior, and they took on LEGO building activities. "They were in these teams and got very competitive," she says with a laugh. "It was so nice to see the difference in the kids after about six weeks. In school, they were really focused and able to concentrate better. It's nice when you know it works." The group even went together to *The Art of the Brick*, an exhibition of art installations made using LEGO bricks by LEGO certified professional Nathan Sawaya. Spending a day out marveling at the creations cemented the bond between the children and the seniors.

While LEGO bricks are part of Kitty's tool kit, all of her work is based on her belief that creativity can build confidence. By encouraging people to be creative and to share their creativity, she believes they will gain confidence in other areas of life. "It allows people to be free," she says. "You could say to somebody, 'Right, you're going to go on stage now and talk,' and they'll shut down, whereas if you give them something creative to do, they are having so much fun they forget about anything else."

Before she got involved with hosting LEGO building sessions, Kitty's main experience with LEGO bricks was cleaning her children's sets off the living room floor. Now, though, she has a different perspective. "The LEGO System is a tool," she says. "It's a universal communication tool that works for everybody—young, old, and in between. That's why it's brilliant." The next stage in Kitty's project supporting seniors is to train others so more nursing homes can benefit from this unique activity. It is vital to the quality of senior residents' lives that they have opportunities to engage with as many different activities as possible—and LEGO bricks are a playful, joyful, and fulfilling part of that mix.

TOP Magnifying glasses can help enlarge building instructions for senior builders who need help seeing element details.

BOTTOM After working with Kitty, senior builders often rediscover their childhood love of LEGO bricks.

ACKNOWLEDGMENTS

Thank you to April Haesler for always being a source of support and encouragement.

A special thank you to Brittany McInerney and Maddy Wong for guiding me through the process of writing this book with constant positivity and enthusiasm.

Thank you to everyone else at Chronicle who made this book happen: Sara Schneider, Christina Amini, Michelle Clair, Becca Boe, Aki Neumann, Natalie Nicolson, and April Whitney. Thank you to MacFadden & Thorpe for their expert design.

Thank you to the team at the LEGO Group for their work on this book: Randi Kirsten Sørensen, Martin Leighton Lindhardt, Tess Howarth, Heidi K. Jensen, Lydia Barram, Amy Jarashow, and Robin James Pearson.

Thank you to Patrick Hoole for conducting the interview with Rita Ebel and to Jay Justice for reviewing the manuscript.

And, most importantly, thank you to everyone who shared their inspiring stories: Dr. Ellen Bronson, Tolgahan Çoğulu, David Clarke, Rita Ebel, Jeff Friesen, Dr. Gina Gómez de la Cuesta and the Play Included team, Dr. Mei Lin Neo, Lauren O'Hara and the LEGO Replay team, Matthew Shifrin, Kitty Short, Stine Storm and the LEGO Braille Bricks team, Caireen Sutherland, Dr. Jani Thuaibah Isa Tanzil, Jan Vormann, and Wei Long Ow Yong.

Photography Credits

All photographs and illustrations © The LEGO Group, except for the following:
Pp 2, 28, 30–31, 33, 35: © 2022 Artists Rights Society (ARS), New York / VG Bild-Kunst, Bonn
Pp 10, 12–16, 19: Carlos Arturo Torres
P 46: Shutterstock, Steve Bower
Pp 48, 51, 53: Maryland Zoo
P 49: Shutterstock, Shiva Photo
Pp 54, 57, 58: Tolgahan Çoğulu
Pp 60–61: Abdullah Sanli
Pp 62, 66: Matthew Shifrin
P 65: Shutterstock, Juan Ci
P 67: Shutterstock, vvoe
Pp 72, 77 (top): Sandra Schildwächter
Pp 74–75, 77 (bottom): Rita Ebel
P 76: Simon Berninger
Pp 80, 83, 85, 86 (top), 87: Jeff Friesen
P 84: Tim Stubbings/Alamy Stock Photo
P 86 (bottom): Peter Harvie/Alamy Stock Photo
P 96: Shutterstock, Ethan Daniels
Pp 98–101: Tropical Marine Science Institute, National University of Singapore, Singapore
Pp 104, 106, 108–109, 111: Natasha Moses